MW01487437

2 CLOWN PLAYS

CAMERON CHRISTOPHER STUART
AND
SERAPHIC ROMANCE ROTS TRUTH

spread it

A FREEDOM BOOK

www.afreedombooks.com

Published by A FREEDOM BOOKS

PUBLISHER'S NOTE
This is a work of fiction. Names, characters, places, and
incidents either are the product of the author's *imagination*
or are used fictitiously, and any resemblance to actual
persons, living or dead, business establishments, events, or
locales is entirely coincidental.

LIBRARY OF CONGRESS CATALOGUING IN PUBLICATION DATA
Stuart, Cameron, 1983-
Clown Plays / Cameron Stuart
p. cm.
ISBN 978-0-9984-2581-8

Printed in the United States of America

to Lily Chambers

Contents

Introduction

Why clowns? There's no particular reason. Sometimes a thought swims by, and you fish it out for lack of anything better happening at the moment. Or you discover that you are a radio and start broadcasting some station you didn't realize was in the air. Orpheus wrote all his poetry by translating the mutterings of a horse. You might try that sometime, it works out pretty well.

Maybe it's where I grew up. Sarasota, Florida is a clown town. The Ringling Brothers circus moved there in the late 1920s and the city I know built up around it. Sarasota is saturated in clown culture, with a clown museum, a clown school, and famous clowns in the graveyards. Clown statues in heroic poses adorn the streets of downtown. I grew up in a tiny blue room decorated with little silver and gold clowns with big smiles, pointy hats on their curly hair, and clasping hands so you could hang them on curtain rods and light fixtures. They would hang about my room and smile. I considered them friends. I love clowns of all varieties: sad clowns, dumb clowns, even scary clowns (but only the fictive ones).

Clowns are unfettered by acceptable decorum. They commit acts and speak words beyond the scope of "normal" day-to-day living. Clowns fail with impunity, as well as succeed. They have the power to bring anyone down to their clown level, including the king. They speak nonsense one moment, and poetry the next. If the immortal line "life is a dream" holds true, and a=b, then b=a and dreams are life. The two are interchangeable, dreams are no less real than school, work, or the hours of my youth I spent glued to the television. This book is a record of dreams as well as events. All of this really happened to us; we really were these clowns night after night. We were never polished, but we were passionate.

I "accidentally" moved back to New York in 2015, deep in the throes of a clown obsession. An opportunity arrived: to stage a new play with my theater company, Saints of an Unnamed Country. I took it, with the condition that no matter what play we did, it would be full of clowns. The only unproduced play I had at that moment was *City of Songs*, written way back in 2012 as a poem of about eight pages about poorly singing cowboys. No matter, I thought. We could do cowboys *as clowns*.

I had only met Lily Chambers a few times, but I knew she was the ideal candidate to become a clown in the theater company. She was a talented actress, we got along, and best of all she had an open schedule. We became roommates, acting partners, and full-time clowns: clown bartenders, clown party guests, clown performers, stumbling and drunk clowns at midnight, clowns deep in the basement of our home, the Bohemian Grove.

Our production of *City of Songs* came and went as spring turned into summer. Bradley Bailey, a close friend, traveling companion, and exceptional performer, visited New York to add his own touch of clown energy. After the show, Bradley departed NYC. But I wasn't done. I wanted more; this clown existence was too much fun to abandon. I wrote another play, this time starring Lily and me as convict clowns. That became "*Jailbreak*!"*tm. Dean Cercone, a visual and sound artist, joined our troop. The three of us made it to Detroit as a clown gang. We performed in our dirty prison outfits in bars, parks, even on the side of a mountain on the shore of the Hudson. We performed at venues throughout our neighborhood of Bushwick, Lily and I hurling insults at each other, screaming about our genitals.

For me, Lily is one of the all-time top clowns. There will never be another clown like her. I can't adequately explain the fun I had on stage with that clown; it was positively addictive. Sadly, I cannot put that clown in this book. All that's left are the scripts, edited and published in this slim volume. Here is the physical record that someone far away can pick up, read, and find useful. They can imagine their own clown, even stage these plays and become clowns themselves. Or be inspired and write their own clown plays.

When we performed these plays, we tried to remain faithful to the words the hand wrote. But plays are not like books. They are very immediate, and we made decisions moment to moment on stage to make our performance work. I added some notes about what was altered and what we improvised. I love to read plays as writing, as poetry. But plays are for changing. Hack them up, reorganize them, stage them in different ways, whatever works. The printed version of these plays are largely transcribed from videos of us performing. In the end, what we found useful as performers mattered most.

I wish I could give you a ticket to one of our shows, and Lily and I would be there performing for you in clown face and attire. Instead, I offer these scripts and a few pictures of us performing, meant to inspire you to slap on a little makeup, pick up a wig, and try out your own clown fantasy. More clowns in every town, I say! To save speech, to wring it dry, the revolution in things is to be found in sound!

Special Thanks: Dean, Bradley, Rebecca, Gina, Bedford and Megan, Stephanie, David Shull, Rachel and Erik Z., Darcey and Kevin, Nyssa and Mike G., Dan Goldberg, Catherine Rush, Nick W., Brett W. Thompson, Ben Grad, Lauren and Mallie, and Marshall James Kavanaugh—and many more.

CITY OF SONGS:
SONGS AGAINST SINGING

City of Songs – Songs Against Singing was first performed by Saints of an Unnamed Country at Secret Project Robot in March, 2015 in a workshop format. It was subsequently performed at Bohemian Grove in April, 2015 for three nights, before returning to Secret Project Robot and Tarot Society in June. All performances were in Bushwick, Brooklyn, and had the following cast:

BILLY THE KIDDER*:	Lily Chambers
JOHN WESLEY HARDIN(G):	Cameron Stuart
GEORGE THE PORTER:	Bradley Bailey
RADIO VOICE:	Rebecca Richards

Directed by Cameron Stuart
Scene Design by Dean Cercone
Original Music by Bradley Bailey & Cast

*Note: BILLY THE KIDDER was played in our production by Lily Chambers as BILLIE THE KIDDER.

Note about the text: The characters sing and play instruments throughout. In general, the singing has been marked with italics and quotation marks, like so:

"Amazing Grace"

BILLY and JOHN are horrible singers. They lack any rhythm or pitch and cannot carry a tune. They are not good at their instruments, and the guitar is always out of tune. The few times they succeed is noted in the text. GEORGE is very talented as a singer, guitarist, and piano player.

Another note about the text: This play was written as a poem to be reconfigured when performed. In the original document, there was no indication of who spoke each line, although in general a rhythm of conversation could sometimes be discerned.

In rehearsal, choices were made about who spoke each line, and that has been notated in this version of the script. In addition, certain parts were added that filled out dramatic shifts. This was done usually with improvised words that changed from night to night. Those parts have also been added and notated, alongside notation of important actions.

Otherwise, the format of the original poem has been retained (somewhat). The final product is a hybrid between readability as a script and the intent behind the work as a poem written for the page.

Scene: A small room, decorated with paintings. One painting depicts a desert. Another depicts an ocean. Or maybe one painting depicts a valley, and the other one depicts some hills. It is hard to tell. In the back is a painting of a railroad track leading off into the sunset. There is a piano as well, and signs of country and western life. A piano bench sits center. The room looks like a cross between a luxury train car and an uncle's basement turned into a practice room for his honky-tonk band.

PROLOGUE

[*GEORGE THE PORTER stands waiting on the platform for ticket holders to arrive. He wears a green hat appropriate for a train worker and has a white clown face with diamond eyes. A voice on the radio floats over the scene, accompanied by canned stride piano, piped in over the stereo.*]

RADIO VOICE: Hello and welcome back to WFLA out of Tallahassee, Florida, your alternative to Federal Broadcasting. Next up, we're going to hear the very first album ever recorded by the famous singing and songwriting duo of Billy Kidder and John W.H.G. You probably recognize the names – they are well known for their recordings of popular Christmas songs. However, you'd never guess how they got their start. Let's take a listen to how they found their voice with their debut recording, Songs Against Singing.

[*Stride piano continues as BILLY THE KIDDER enters with hobo knapsack. BILLY is overwhelming blue in attire, wears tights, a western shirt, and a cowboy hat. He has a white clown face with a painted blue Zanni-style mask. He hands GEORGE a ticket and a demo tape. He is admitted into the train car. He leaves his knapsack in the back and takes a seat on the piano bench. JOHN WESLEY HARDIN(G) enters next. JOHN wears red tights, a white western shirt, and a flat brim black hat. He has a white clown face with a painted red Zanni-style mask. He gives GEORGE his ticket, followed by a demo tape. JOHN carries his guitar and suitcase into the train car. Oblivious, JOHN pushes BILLY aside and sits legs spread apart and wielding his guitar on the opposite side of the piano bench. GEORGE takes a seat by the piano as the stride piano fades out. BILLY takes out a harmonica and blasts a few chords. JOHN is astonished. He looks over, causing BILLY to stop. JOHN strums a few out of tune chords. BILLY is mesmerized. He looks over, causing JOHN to stop. Suddenly, they break into a guitar and harmonica duet, which continues on badly, until stopped by their laughter.]*

[improvised]
JOHN WESLEY HARDIN(G): Well that sounded pretty good there, mister. Exactly where is someone such as yourself headed now?
BILLY THE KIDDER: It's very funny you'd ask me that, sir, because I am an extraordinarily talented singer and songwriter and I'm headed to the **CITY OF SONGS**.
JOHN WESLEY HARDIN(G): Well you don't say. Well I am also an extraordinarily talented singer and songwriter and I am also headed – to the **CITY OF SONGS**.
BILLY THE KIDDER: Well shit Goddammit!

[BILLY and JOHN launch into a train rhythm on their instruments. GEORGE pulls out a cardboard cutout of a train. He circles BILLY and JOHN in rhythm with the instruments. As the moment passes, GEORGE sits down at the piano, puts away the train cutout, and retrieves a guitar. GEROGE accompanies the action on his guitar throughout the scenes, playing both under and with the action, speaking, and singing of BILLY and JOHN. GEORGE only stops his accompaniment when he returns in Track Seven.]

RADIO VOICE: Track 1 – Billy and John Form a
                              Songwriting Partnership

[*improvised*]
JOHN: Alright buddy – if you're a singer, I gotta hear them
pipes man, gotta hear 'em –
BILLY: "*Welcome to the City*"
JOHN: Death to the City!
BILLY: "*the City of Songs*"
JOHN: Death to all Songs!

[*Attention reverses.*]

JOHN: "*Welcome to the City*"
BILLY: Death to the City!
JOHN: "*the City of Songs*"
BILLY: Death to the singers!
BOTH: Death and damnation to all!

[*Instruments disappear/are put away.*]

JOHN: Nothing but a couple of outlaws –
BILLY: writers and poets –
JOHN: gunslingers –
BILLY: wanders –
JOHN: trouble if I ever saw it!

BILLY: Shine a light on 'em.

[*An overhead light comes on.*]

BILLY: My name is
              Billy
              the
              Kidder

JOHN: *"Billy the Kid*
Look what he did"

BILLY: First time I heard that name, it was on a record, a record I found hanging on a wall in a dusty beat down ol' dime store...

JOHN: *"I'll sing you a song of Billy the Kid"*

BILLY: and I stole that name, and with it a face, and now I won't rest until that song is my song, until that story is a living breathing prophecy

JOHN: *"I'll sing of the desperate deeds that he did"*

JOHN: My name is
John
Wesley
Hardin(g) – with or without the G as you please.

BILLY: *"A gun in his hand*
A woman in his bed"

JOHN: First time I heard that name, a man was singing it – but that name didn't belong to him – he stole that name and he stuffed it in a song and he started singing it just to glorify himself...

BILLY: *"He was always known to lend a helping hand"*

JOHN: I stole that name back – cuz it belongs to an outlaw, not some rich, white dandy motherfucker, some pussy ass singer. It belongs to a killer!

BILLY: *"He stole from the rich and gave to the poor"*

[Before BILLY can finish, JOHN chokes BILLY for a moment, demonstrating his credentials as a killer, before returning to reality.]

[Light turns off.]

BILLY: We stole those songs from the singers and their sellers and now we wander this land singing their songs all wrong

JOHN: If you can't stop the songs
        stop the singers

BILLY: Stop the singing
        overload the lungs
        cut off the circulation

JOHN: We come to this city
BILLY: – death to this city! –
JOHN: we come bearing OUR songs

BILLY: Songs against songs
JOHN: Songs against singing

BOTH: An outlaw literature!

JOHN: No songs
BILLY: no singing
JOHN: only sound
BILLY: only emptying our bodies of air
        again and again
JOHN: emptying ourselves of your wicked city's air
BILLY: the dark pollution of your sanctified
JOHN: over saturated
BILLY: city

BOTH: Boom!
JOHN: We gonna string up your singers by the throat!

[*JOHN chokes BILLY for a moment, then releases him, embarrassed. The two walk into a painting of a railroad track.*]

RADIO VOICE: Track 2 – Words and Music,
the Marriage of

[*BILLY and JOHN with their instruments, trying to write songs.
BILLY has a notebook.*]

BILLY: The songs all start somewhere,
JOHN: before you ever heard them...

BILLY: *"Motherless children have a hard time"*

JOHN: *"Don't the moon look pretty
I can see her but she can't see me"*

BILLY: The songs trace back to the past,
JOHN: to the beginning
BILLY: Eros
JOHN: myth weaver

[*JOHN, confused this as a signal, puckers up, looking for a kiss. BILLY
slaps him.*]

BILLY: *"We will all go to meet him when he comes,*
JOHN: *we will all go to meet him when he comes,*
BOTH: *we will all go to meet him
when the bridegroom comes"*

BILLY: The bride
on her wedding day
all dressed in white
JOHN: and the singer lives on, hidden in the song
like in a coat, or some brambles or some shit

BILLY: *"We will all bring the flour when he comes,*
JOHN: *we will all bring the flour when he comes,*

BOTH: *we will all bring the flour*
           when the bridegroom comes"

[*BILLY and JOHN kneel to pray.*]

BILLY: [*mumbling, improvised*] Jesus Christ ... I've been a bad little boy ... I know I've fucked up ... I didn't mean to ... thanks for looking out for me ... amen.
JOHN: [*mumbling at the same time, improvised*] Dear Satan ... please let me lick your hairy goat balls ... and give me the power to seduce 14-year-old girls with my skill at guitar ...

[*JOHN leaps up and snatches his guitar, playing along.*]

JOHN: *"Don't the moon look pretty*
           I can see her but she can't see me"

BILLY: The singer ushers her on
           her song, like a rose-tinged star,
           her song,
           raises high the beams of the raftered hall

JOHN: Writing is often done late at night, so they can't see you sinning

[*Instruments disappear, drinking of bourbon begins.*]

BILLY: We shall tear it down
JOHN: We shall tear down the walls of this city
BILLY: We shall tear down their raftered hall
JOHN: We shall dissolve the weave
BILLY: Eros, dissolves all.

[*JOHN chokes BILLY.*]

BILLY: *"Oh the Virgin Lee,*
   oh the Virgin Lee,
   why you done gone, leaving me?"

[*BILLY is released, annoyed but pleased with the results of singing while being choked. After recovering, BILLY chokes JOHN.*]

JOHN: *"Oh the Virgin Lee,*
   oh the Virgin Lee,
   do I still yearn for my Mary Lee?"

[*JOHN is released, his shock giving way to astonishment at his singing's sincerity.*]

BILLY: [*with notebook*] Writing should be done in the dead of the night – when my spirit is wet with moonlight, when my heart is full of venom and poison, the blackest bile...

JOHN: I've come to sing a song against the record, against
   the beginning, against the origin of love,
   against his story
   I sing a song of bodies dissolving
   no singers
   only our bodies dissolved into sound

BILLY: Untangle the weave
JOHN: Liars all
BILLY: You don't know the man
   only the myth
JOHN: This bridegroom comes bearing
   the songs against songs
   the songs against singing

[*BILLY and JOHN walk into a painting of a railroad track.*]

RADIO VOICE: Track 3 – Choreography for my enemy, my very own record collection, aka the Book of Songs

[*JOHN has a tape recorder. He puts on a tape they've made of their songs.*]

JOHN: I begin by recording bird calls
        wandering through the field
        with nothing but a tape recorder
BILLY: Now a bird's got a song to sing
        sparrow and nightingale
JOHN: I sneak up real close
        and press record

[*Tape begins. Guitar and harmonica throughout tape. GEORGE silent. BILLY and JOHN pantomime to the songs on the tape. Following dialogue indicates the voices on the recording.*]

[*BILLY tries to bond with JOHN through exercise, meditation, and yoga. JOHN is more interested in practicing his air guitar skills.*]

      JOHN: *"Imma thousand miles from nowhere*
      BILLY: *in a one horse town*
      JOHN: *gravestone for a pillow*
      BILLY: *fairgrounds for a bed"*

      JOHN: *"dig my grave with a silver spade*
      BILLY: *and promise me you gonna keep that grave clean"*

[*JOHN breaks out a flask of bourbon. BILLY partakes, and they end up playing leap frog.*]

      JOHN: I make a record of the song the bird sang
                   a song is anything you can sing
                   leaps up outta the lungs

              changes the air
              fills up the room

BILLY: *"I am a man of constant sorrow*
           I shiver inside the season of winter
           And I carve out a living in a wooden hallow"

[BILLY takes a glass pipe from his satchel. JOHN, nervous, joins him. They smoke weed until thoroughly stoned, then sip more from the flask.]

JOHN: Given over to exaggeration
         this animal, lost
         deep in the wilderness
         retracts his claws
         and sinks deep into the weeds
         his body wracked with pain

[BILLY and JOHN slip on headphones to better examine their singing on the tape.]

BOTH: *"Heart beating like a hammer*
         Eyes full of tears" *[repeats]*

[Disgusted by their lack of talent, BILLY and JOHN blame each other, and then leave the room.]

JOHN: Blond decisions
         the song is a rope
         I slice open my own neck
         with my chapped open palms

[BILLY and JOHN return. They take out their record collection and start smashing all the vinyl. They jump up and down on the broken bits.]

BILLY: *"You been gone for only hours"*
JOHN: *"You been gone"*
BILLY: *"But for me one million years"*

[*BILLY finds a record they both still love. Instead of smashing it, BILLY and JOHN put it on.*]

JOHN: He sings himself out of existence
          once you have the record
          you make it into a book
          one of the classics, the book of songs
          an annotated collection, a record album

[*The record comes on. It's a great rendition of a country blues number by the Lemon Kid. BILLY and JOHN listen in delight.*]

RECORD: *"White moon is rising tonight*

[*The record is interrupted by a version of BILLY and JOHN doing the number. They are horrible.*]

BILLY: *"Deep in the midnight hour*
          I watch her from my tower
          until my heart is devoured"

[*Upset, BILLY and JOHN smash the record, smash everything, fight, choke each other, cry, defecate, vomit, die, yet still the song goes on, their voices upsetting – until finally they plug their ears with fingers and it stops.*]

JOHN: I want to sing
      but I will not sing another man's song

BILLY: Will you sing your own song?

JOHN: Like A Song of Myself? [*improvised*] And we can be called the Leaves of Grass!

BILLY: No!

JOHN: Fine! – I will not sing

BILLY: No – you will be sung.

[*BILLY and JOHN walk into a painting of a railroad track.*]

RADIO VOICE: Track 4 – America

[*BILLY with notebook, JOHN with guitar, writing words and music.
BILLY refers to the paintings throughout.*]

BILLY: Ocean
JOHN: *"In the ocean there's a desert,"*
BILLY: Desert
JOHN: *"in the desert there's a war."*
BILLY: Thine inland seas, gems among the oceans
JOHN: *"In my mind there's an ocean,"*
BILLY: Rocks and rills of the sparkling sandy desert
JOHN: *"in my country's desert there's a war."*

BILLY: In the desert there are vultures
          inside the vulture there are bones.

JOHN: *"These answers you'll find in a book,"*

BILLY: and you cook down the bones to get the gold,
          song gold real nice for writing songs

JOHN: *"hidden in every dresser drawer."*

[*JOHN reads from BILLY's notebook.*]

JOHN: What a fine day
          desert over here full of vultures, carrion teeth I'd like
          to pick clean [*discards notebook*]
          Put it over a spigot
          embrace all, embrace all and empty out

BILLY: Mountain
JOHN: *"I climbed up a mountain,"*
BILLY: Valley

JOHN: *"slept on the valley floor."*
BILLY: Purple mountains, wild and steep
JOHN: *"My chest became that mountain,"*
BILLY: Fruited plains leading to an endless golden valley
JOHN: *"my head resting 'gainst the valley floor."*

BILLY: Mountains populated by a confederation of trees
      whole choirs of trees

JOHN: *"These answers you'll find in a book,"*

BILLY: Trees too busy in their pursuit of time
      to ever be sung into a city

JOHN: *"hidden in every dresser drawer."*
      [*without guitar*]
      The river valley floods every year
      water rises up to the throats of the singers
      I wade out up to my knees and call their names

      [*without notebook*]
BILLY: If I don't understand my body
      how can I know this country?

      [*with guitar*]
JOHN: *"America*
      America
      the beautiful
      the beautiful"

      First time I heard that word
      it was in a song

BILLY: Which word?

JOHN: You didn't listen
      I sang the same word twice

[*BILLY and JOHN walk into a painting of a railroad track.*]

RADIO VOICE: Track 5 – Cannonball – a train of thought

[*JOHN tries to remember a song he once heard. BILLY eggs him on with harmonica.*]

JOHN: You remember that one song
       long black railroad car

BILLY: Trains moving through here all the time

JOHN: *"This Train I ride"*
       [*searching for words and melody*]
BOTH: [*improvised*] *"22? 50? 17? Sixteen!"*

BILLY: This train is got ghosts tacked to the walls
       their heads split wide open with railway ties

BILLY: [*with harmonica*] *"This Train I ride"*
       [*searching for words and melody*]
BOTH: [*improvised*] *"Sixteen rabbits? Buttercups? What was it?"*

JOHN: Sitting here, bottle of heaven in each hand
       Straight. Kentucky. Bourbon.

JOHN: [*with bourbon*] *"This Train I ride"*
       [*searching for words and melody*]
BOTH: [*improvised*] *"Sixteen coaches!"*

BILLY: You remember that one tune?
JOHN: How does it go?
BILLY: Starts off on a real high note... [*harmonica high note*]

BOTH: *"This Train I ride*
       16 coaches stretching 900 miles long"

[*having found it, they continue onward*]
JOHN: and then it gets weird
BILLY: sound of saws grinding
JOHN: and flies buzzing around a corpse

BILLY: Hey remember that one song
       How does it go?
JOHN: It starts off reaaaal slow
BILLY: and then
       gets
       real fast
       train clopping like a misshod horse

JOHN: Faces hidden in the windows driven through by soft
       nails
BILLY: instruments hiding out in the corners
JOHN: tongues caressing the underside of the carriage
BILLY: pierced through by the dagger of thought
JOHN: thin as light itself
BILLY: and then dragged loose!

JOHN: Melody only a fraction of a song
BILLY: change one word –
JOHN: the train comes loose, spins off the track

JOHN: And we trade cars
BILLY: Hiding out in an empty railway car
JOHN: Jack of Diamonds
BILLY: Queen of Hearts
JOHN: We pluck the stars from the moon's eyes
BILLY: We wear a veil of darkness, and hide in a crowded
       room
JOHN: We eat our organs, consume our hearts and survive
BILLY: We dream the perfect poem
JOHN: and then we forget it

BOTH: THE TRAIN STOPS!

[*with aplomb and a semblance of a melody*]
BOTH: *"Train I ride don't burn on coal*
        train I write called the cannonball"

[*improvised*]
JOHN: That's what we should be called! The cannons!
BILLY: The balls!
JOHN: We'll work on that!
BILLY: Come on!

[*BILLY and JOHN walk into a painting of a railroad track.*]

RADIO VOICE: Track 6 – Bottom of the Well

[*The moon, a broken piece of vinyl, descends. An overhead light illuminates the moon.*]

JOHN: They exhibit a sensitivity to light...
BILLY: We've been living off moonlight

[*The light falls. Scared, they hide beneath the furniture.*]

BILLY: A monster lives beneath the bridge
         down in the basement
JOHN: You want to close it in, keep it in the ground
         but it opens up
BOTH: Open, open, open all

[*They emerge.*]
JOHN: Something lurks
BILLY: un derground
JOHN: un restricted
BILLY: and un frozen
JOHN: un folding
BILLY: un woven
JOHN: un necessary
BILLY: and un packed

[*They dance real slow, in a circle, with guitar and harmonica, singing a song they suddenly receive. It's pretty good, although really weird. They still can't sing or play, but it's eerie albeit naïve.*]

JOHN: "*Lay down your weary hands*
       I've been working"

[*speaking in rhythm*]
BILLY: "*writing the physical backwards*
      I'd a monster with no teeth"

JOHN: un lingual
BILLY: un terranean

[*Instruments disappear. They yawn, and collect upstage to sleep.*]

BOTH: "*Deep down*
      down the old well
      a well with no bottom
      bottomless well
      a bottomless well"

[*Now sitting back to back, they sing themselves to sleep.*]

BOTH: "*Deep down*
      down the old well
      a well with no bottom
      bottomless well
      a bottomless well" [*trails off*]

[*They each stand in turn, speaking in a dream, only to return to sleeping, sitting and snoring below.*]

BILLY: The singer's voice is the tale – found here – in the un natural moonlight un folding un derground – my lungs two cups filled to the brim with ether, morphine spilling from my lips. Un cover red desire, hidden beneath my tongue, aflame with righteous fire, un natural organs un done by sound, strung out strands on a heart's loom. I'm drunk on moonlight, on the ocean's call. These words haunted, not only by his story, but with my desire, which exceeds all y'alls languages.

JOHN: In the city (my father's city) he hung his dusty old hat right where the poem began – wires holding it together, all through the brim. "Why you a singer?" The answering call came from the woods, like a train whistle bounced back by satellite. And now my turn will come, stage un lit, while the moon bows un der an ocean of rough red crystal, sweet ribbons damp against her brow, un woven the un born are, and the singer's voice scuttles like a shuttle across the empty space of the loom of the mind.

[*Tableau as BILLY and JOHN sleep.*]

RADIO VOICE: Track 7 – Porter's Song

[*GEORGE finds BILLY and JOHN asleep on the floor, still back to back.*]

GEORGE: Wake up!

BILLY: Hello George!
JOHN: Hello George!
GEORGE: [*with demo tapes*]
        Now I've looked at your songs. You say
        you want to be let in
        into the City of Songs
        and you come bearing these outlaw songs.
        Obviously – we judge the content of the song.
        But we also take a look at the singer.

BOTH: These are songs against the singer!

GEORGE: Now you say you've written songs
        you can't help but sing wrong,
        Imma gonna tell you two
        it can't be wrong.

[*GEORGE hands them the guitar. The harmonica appears. They accompany themselves.*]
BILLY: "*Standing on the platform*
JOHN: *smoking cheap cigars*"

GEORGE: If there's a record of it – that's the way the song is and it can't be any other way – we can hold it in our hands and know it, know what it is. The record of the song IS the song and it repeats and it's never wrong.

BILLY: "*While the porter reads our papers*
JOHN: *We're strumming our guitars*"

GEORGE: That's how ya get hits. It's either a classic
        or it ain't.
        See, the only way into this city
        is if you sing yourself into it –
        And the songs make the singers.

BILLY: *"Good morning Mr. Railroad Man,*
JOHN: *you found us hiding in an empty car"*

GEORGE: Songs make singers immortal
        Songs got to be sung.

BILLY: *"We're traveling to the city*
JOHN: *Writing songs un derneath the stars"*

[*GEORGE, disgusted, snatches the guitar away from JOHN and silences BILLY's harmonica.*]

GEORGE: Now not everyone can sing
        Sure anyone can make a sound
        but singing is something people WANT to hear
        We're trying to make hits here boys!
        The melody is just part of the songs
        and a song is more than just the structure
        you got to bring it alive with singing

[*BILLY and JOHN make disgusting sounds, like dying animals or babies, in their sad imitation of singing.*]

GEORGE: So – you got any hits?

BILLY: I've been to the bottom of the ocean
JOHN: I've been in the love with the moon

GEORGE: Let me tell you something
        Your words aren't gonna make a difference

inside the City
they've got a library
every word ever said
started off in a song
every story ever told
started with someone singing.
None of this is yours.
It is all in there, already inside

[*GEORGE finds his way to the piano. He begins singing a song of songs.*]

GEORGE: *"Cowboys, Indians, pirates, lawyers,"*

[*GEORGE begins playing the piano. The expert rhythm takes control of BILLY and JOHN, and they find themselves beginning to dance.*]

GEORGE: *"Work songs, death songs, marriage songs, love songs*
Prison songs, road songs, blues songs, gospels songs,
Rags, tunes, ballads, boogies,
Country and western songs, wagon songs, traditional songs,
holiday songs, CHRISTMAS SONGS"

[*The tempo increases. BILLY and JOHN are marionettes on invisible strings, dancing to the rhythm in the melody.*]

GEORGE: *"Songs about women, songs about trains,*
songs about war and your brother,
songs about JESUS!"

[*BILLY and JOHN, having danced into a crucifix pose, are released from the song and shake it out.*]

GEORGE: All of it – inside.

BILLY: Yeah? Well, what's outside?
GEORGE: Outside?
JOHN: Yeah! Outside the city, outside the walls

GEORGE: Well – maybe there's a highway. Yes, a road, a long, winding road, bringing would be singers clamoring to get into the city.

BILLY: OK, but where's the road go,
           where's that coming from?
JOHN: Yeah, like, what doesn't make its way into a song?
GEORGE: I suppose from time to time
           Someone tries to bring something from outside
           into the City of Songs.
           However everything in the City of Songs
           already belongs
           so I suppose I could not say,
           say quite for sure
           what's outside the city

JOHN: I'll tell you what it is. It's the opposite of his story
           the un his story.
BILLY: It's like how you can put a tree into a song
           but you can't turn a tree into a singer
GEORGE: Sure, there are whole choirs of trees

JOHN: They may be singing, but they aren't singers,
           because you can't steal their songs.
BILLY: Boom!

[*A flask appears. GEORGE is bewildered. They all drink.*]

GEORGE: I think you're ready.
JOHN: Hot Dog!

RADIO VOICE: Track 8 – Billy and John's Christmas Single

GEORGE: Now the final test –
        Join me in a song.

[*They collect downstage. BILLY and JOHN kneel and fold their hands.
GEORGE assumes the posture of a choir director.*]

GEORGE: A song my mother used to sing me
        (my father never sang)

ALL: *"Silent night holy night*
        All is calm all is bright
        'Round yon virgin mother and child
        Holy infant so tender and mild
        Sleep in heavenly peace
        Sleep in heavenly peace"

BILLY: And then the porter
        reaches into the sky
        and picks up the moon
        like it's a small wafer of bread
        and he breaks it into three pieces
        one for you, one for you,
        and one for me

[*So it is, happening just as described. They eat the pieces of the vinyl
moon.*]

JOHN: And the walls of the city tremble
        walls long and wide, gilded and gold

[*A spontaneous jam begins, GEORGE on piano, BILLY on harmonica,
and JOHN grabs his guitar.*]

JOHN: timber of shellac, vinyl, and plastic
      acetate and paper
      stacked long and high
      and the gates creak open
      the gates to the City of Songs!

GEORGE: Welcome, welcome and congratulations,
      come in my friends.

[*BILLY and JOHN are elated at their victory. They all shake hands.*]

GEORGE: You've made it to the City of Songs
      You're singers now and so join us
      You've climbed up on the first rung of the ladder
      welcome to the City of Songs
      welcome to eternity
      place of heaven, or home to misery

[*BILLY and JOHN pack their things, bid adieu to each other and GEORGE, and leave in opposite directions.*]

JOHN: *"Welcome to the city*
      I'll be singing every night"
BILLY: *"Isn't it a pity*
      Gonna sing away my life."

[*Exeunt all.*]
[*Canned stride piano returns, piped in over stereo.*]

RADIO VOICE: Songs against Singing – Billy and John's first album – is a forgotten classic, now reissued on Swamptown records. Buy it now and receive a commemorative button. It's your chance to own part of history – Billy and John are such an unforgettable part of the American story, it would be a travesty to forget how they began. Nowadays, one is a senator, and the other is a preacher. But we can never forget their early motto – To Save Speech, To Wring it Dry. The Revolution in Things is to be Found in Sound. This is WFLA, signing off. Ghost mother infiltrated by paroxysms of death swallow spirittalk radio garbage surviving material feedback of diverted genesis. I dissemble my machine and vanish. Goodnight y'all!

CURTAIN

Photos of *City of Songs* at Bohemian Grove in Bushwick, Brooklyn on May 1st, 2nd, and 3rd, 2015.

All Photos by Brett W. Thompson except for opposite page, photo by Lauren Spencer.

Photos from "_Jailbreak_!"*tm at Bohemian Grove in
Bushwick, Brooklyn, October 1st, 2nd, 3rd, and 4th.

All pictures by Ben Grad | bengrad.com.

"<u>Jailbreak</u>!"*tm

"Jailbreak!"*tm was produced by Saints of an Unnamed
Country in 2015. It was workshopped in August at Sonny's
Bar in Pittsburgh, Trinosophes in Detroit, and Secret Project
Robot in Brooklyn in August, 2015. It was performed on the
banks of the Hudson near Mount Taurus in Cold Spring, NY
in early September, before receiving a four-day run at
Bohemian Grove in Brooklyn as part of a performance
festival in October. Additional performances in November
happened at the Living Gallery in Brooklyn and a final bow
at the Big Haus in Atlanta. All these performances had the
following cast:

LULU THE LUNATIC: Lily Chambers
KOKO MAGNIFIQUE*:   Cameron Stuart
SOUND PERSON: Dean Cercone
TELEVISION PERSONALITY: Rebecca Richards

Directed by Cameron Stuart
Scene and Sound Design by Dean Cercone

*Note: Played in our production by Cameron Stuart, a cis
male, KOKO has a fluid gender and exhibits characteristics
of being both male and female at the same time, regardless
of the gender identification of whoever plays her (she does
prefer the pronoun her).

Scene: A dirty room, devoid of furnishings or accents. In the background, a painting of a scene of a city, rife with pollution, police officers, toxic spills, and prison walls. It is rendered in black, white, piss yellow, and vomit green, with accents of red for the sirens. It smells like urine. Downstage across the lip of the stage is a blue banner with painted waves to resemble the ocean. There are two paintings of seashells on either side of the stage. Another painted blue sheet runs from the painting, off the side next to a depiction of a sewer pipe, downstage right to the banner that represents the ocean. In this side river is a stick and some detritus and trash.

[Two figures are kneeling center stage. They have black hoods over their bowed heads, and are handcuffed to each other at opposing wrists. They wear prison garb with painted black stripes on their white prison clothes. Stage left, SOUND PERSON sits secluded with a device for manipulating the sounds. He is always present throughout the action of the play. The two figures are utterly silent and still as SOUND PERSON blasts the voice of TELEVISION PERSONALITY along with canned music appropriate for a news program.]

TELEVISION PERSONALITY: This Just In on Emergency News Updates: Two notorious criminals are on the loose after a high stakes prison escape. Drug kingpin Mikhail Garcia has managed to break out of prison for the second time, apparently with the help of professional rapist slash pedophile Johnny Reb Whitem. Their harrowing 77 hour and 69 minute escape involved possible help from corrupt prison officials, although the only known tools so far are a used diaper and a pair of matched crocodile teeth. Local, state, and federal authorities are working in tandem, in real time, to recover these dangerous threats to society. They are believed to be lingering somewhere outside of your city's borders in an un mapped wilderness zone. Please be advised! Be Extra Ordinarily cautious if you happen to fall outside of the limits of your normal routine into an unfamiliar and perhaps even ethnic neighborhood. These criminals will stop at nothing to infringe upon your liberty!

[*The two figures pull the bags off their heads to reveal LULU, stage left and handcuffed on the right arm, and KOKO, stage right and handcuffed on the left arm. Both have painted clown faces, and both wear white blindfolds. They stand simultaneously and begin running for their lives. They never move an inch from center stage, their legs running pell-mell in an imitation of a cartoon.*]

KOKO: [*stops running for a moment*] Jesus Mother Fucking Holy Crap Christ on a Cracker and Mother Mary Shitter of God!

[*SOUND PERSON cues canned laughter. LULU and KOKO continue to run.*]

LULU: [*stops running for a moment*] Keep running! Keep digging! Keep pushing! We're almost there!

[*SOUND PERSON cues canned laughter. LULU and KOKO continue to run.*]

KOKO: [*stops running for a moment*] Today is the day! The day of our final escape! This is a Jailbreak Trademark season one series finale! Born from a lake of fire, and digging toward the light!

[*SOUND PERSON cues canned laughter. LULU and KOKO continue to run.*]

LULU: [*stops running for a moment*] Stick to our plan, sister! Step 1 – escape! Step 2 – achieve absolute liberty for all eternity! Don't look back at Eurydice!
KOKO: [*stops running for a moment*] Your old city, bitch!

[*SOUND PERSON cues canned cheering and applause. LULU and KOKO continue to run. SOUND PERSON blasts them with another round of TELEVISION PERSONALITY, this time accompanied by canned music from a sitcom.*]

TELEVISION PERSONALITY: Next up on the Network: The latest episode of "Jailbreak!"* Trademark! Returning in its eighth season, with an Emmy nominated cast, it's a "can't miss" premiere special with a seventeen-part story arc! Stay still folks, this one is gonna be a doozie, floozie, badadabambaloozie! Whee! Free TV on Netflix stream service device-ease!

[*KOKO and LULU winded, fall to the ground, catching themselves on all fours. They pull off and discard their blindfolds, revealing painted black bands across their faces, giving them the appearance of a clown crossed with a cat burglar. SOUND PERSON cues the sound of waves crashing on a beach, which persist throughout the remainder of the action.*]

KOKO: Is this the place?
LULU: I dunno. I recognize it...
KOKO: Recognize it?
LULU: Yes. The ... glowing trash. There. And the uh ... what do you see?
KOKO: Water. Lots of water.
LULU: Can you swim?
KOKO: No. Can you?
LULU: Yes.

[*A short moment passes.*]

LULU: Get out the map.
KOKO: It's not a map.
LULU: Get it out.

[KOKO *pulls out "the map" from a hidden pocket. "The map" is actually a crinkled and abused take-out menu from a Chinese restaurant. KOKO begins to read it aloud.*]

KOKO: Lunch special, fried rice with –
LULU: Other side!

[*KOKO flips "the map" to reveal large handwritten instructions.*]

KOKO: "The big score! A bunch of goodies for the badies!
        Crime out! Crime in! A crime that subsists on
        rhyme!"
        What is this shit, Lulu?

LULU: Keep reading!

KOKO: "Beyond the edge of the shore
        Liberty is waiting for ye
        Break free and be
        with us on the island of Mu."
        We are on a beach.
        You took us to a beach.

LULU: Yes. [*pause*] Ok, fine. Look I'm ready to part ways.
KOKO: Ok. Good. I'll go this way.

[*KOKO and LULU attempt to leave in contrary directions.*]

LULU: Unh! No this way.
KOKO: Jesus Christ! This again!
LULU: There it is again – Jesus that Jesus this.
KOKO: Shut up, it's just a word.
LULU: And yet you are so attached.
KOKO: Fuck off! Attached only to you, but not by choice.
Seven goddamn years!

LULU: Seven, Seventeen, Seventeen hundred, floating decimal...

KOKO: Seven years in a manacle!

LULU: MAN-acle. Nice choice of words.

KOKO: Look, we need a plan.

LULU: Got it. Writing. [*pulls pen from bra*] Pen – the planning tool.

KOKO: No, like, plan we need food – Jesus, I'm hungry.

LULU: I can't think when I'm full.

KOKO: I can't think when I'm hungry.

LULU: You can't think at all! No one can. We don't need food. Not where we're going.

KOKO: No food!?

LULU: Nope – no thinking.

KOKO: No thinking!?

LULU: Thinking is colonization of the mind.

KOKO: Only thinking in words! You never change, never give up.

LULU: You always come back. Well. [*Shakes manacle.*] To talking to me.

[*SOUND PERSON cues a harsh industrial sound mixed with the crash of a modem connection and the pounding of machines. Perhaps the sound emanates from the painting of the factory. LULU and KOKO cover their eyes in pain until it passes, about 10 seconds.*]

[*LULU and KOKO are standing. Their predicament has not changed.*]

LULU: Substantive analysis of the matter at hand.

KOKO: We're lost and time is running out.

LULU: Time! – measured or unmeasured?

KOKO: Time – either we get caught or we starve to death! Lost – I dunno, in the wilderness!

LULU: Yes. Lost among the bones and the carnivores... Itemize the action.

KOKO: First, we eat. Preferably meat. Water too.

LULU: Perhaps it'll rain? We could open our little gullets, choke it down, little sky tears.

KOKO: Mmm, some water down the back of my throat.

LULU: Wait! So you place before out liberty mere sustenance? Liberty above all else, for this is our day, to really break free, and do you know what that means?

KOKO: Skip it! I'm not going to stay attached to your ass, dragging you across the beach once you succumb to starvation. [*pause*] Now, what do we got here?

[*KOKO takes a moment to look around the beach, dragging LULU along. Improvisation of discovery such as, "Look at this crappy set!", or "I found a guy wearing a Yankees hat in the front row!", or "There's lots of dirt!" Eventually she finds a stick and returns her attention to LULU.*]

KOKO: Look! A stick.

[*LULU remains unimpressed.*]

KOKO: [*Noticing the set*] I see some seashells.

[*LULU hums the bassline from the Seashellz "Substance to Substance."*]

KOKO: Hmm... Maybe we can catch a seagull and cook it up and eat it. Oh! How about this? [*holds stick appropriately*] Fishing rod.

LULU: You need a line.

KOKO: Oh Oh Oh I got it!

[*KOKO puts her hands in her pants and seemingly retrieves an object from either her pussy or anus.*]

KOKO: Dental floss!

LULU: You need a hook. And bait.

KOKO: I should tear out your tongue.

LULU: Ah ah ah.

KOKO: Come here, I'm gonna tear out your chipped tooth and hang your eye on it.

LULU: Let go of me!

[*KOKO lunges at LULU, with a view at retrieving either a tongue or eye. LULU punches KOKO in her belly. A moment of recognition as KOKO reels from the blow. KOKO recovers.*]

KOKO: Ok. I'm gonna hang this pole out. Wait to see what the world offers.

[*KOKO begins to fish from a seated position, her arm hanging mid-air via handcuff from the still standing arm of LULU.*]

LULU: Bad choice. We need a plan.

KOKO: You work on that. Imma wait for a fishy.

LULU: You are forever caught in a digression toward manifestation.

KOKO: Oh yeah? How about I don't believe you exist. You're a phantom here to torture me.

LULU: You are like a weak magician. You rely on sight, so you think only in illusion.

KOKO: I am an escape artist and an arsonist and you are just a spoiled political writer. Who is the weak fucking link in the chain?

LULU: I mean to really escape! Rather to only make appear or disappear.

KOKO: Your words are like smoke screen for thoughts you don't even have.

LULU: Thinking only in thoughts sculpted in words of antiquity whose grammar is isomorphic to the bouncing unwashed balls of the prison guards and their pewter grey clipped beards. Rapists, twice over! My pussy, my mind!

[*SOUND PERSON cues a harsh industrial sound mixed with the crash of a modem connection and the pounding of machines. Perhaps the sound emanates from the painting of the factory. LULU and KOKO cover their eyes in pain until it passes, about 10 seconds.*]

[*KOKO is seated and fishing. LULU is crouched beside her, writing on "the map."*]

LULU: They'll come along. We'll see a boat.

[*A moment passes in silence.*]

KOKO: Alright, I'll bite. Tell me a story, Lulu.

LULU: Ok. Not a story, but an entry point into the struggle. Slow-mo view of historical change. Liberty as the defining concept of human life, visibly emergent as a growing concern embedded in slave songs giving birth to popular music styles. Which side you on? Butter side up or butter side down?

KOKO: I take it back, I don't want to hear a story.

LULU: This isn't his story. This is the engine of change. I'm talking about liberty! Forget your stories.
KOKO: It's a fucking chore.
LULU: What?
KOKO: Even trying to talk to you.
LULU: Well it's a chore to express myself in these words, normalized by subject predicate relations.
KOKO: It's a chore for everyone on this planet to listen to your terrible poetry!
LULU: On this planet maybe. In this world. Resounding mirrors turn translated currents into dust, alchemical sign.

KOKO: Come on. This is a jailbreak, trademark! This is your time to leave it all behind. Think about it. How did *you* [*points at the pathetic and frail LULU*] – end up in the clink?

LULU: An endless crime. [*Pause.*] Revolt on grammar. [*Pause.*] Liberation of my sphincter to reveal a second tongue. [*Pause. KOKO thinks this last concept is gag worthy.*] My politics.

KOKO: There ya go, some straight talk sister.

LULU: I'm not your sister. We are not sisters. My sisters are in jail. We will remember my sisters or we won't but you are not among them. [*quietly*] You fucking clownie.

KOKO: What the fuck did you just say?

LULU: Nothing.

KOKO: Goddammit right you said nothing – you biotch.

LULU: [*moving on*] Prison. Yes. Ok. It was the revolution. I was part of the revolution.

KOKO: And here you are on the beach waiting for them to pick you up and take you back. You just want to go down the same road twice? This is a jailbreak, trademark! Liberty? I'll say liberty! Let's get all the way out! [*KOKO makes a face to demonstrate how far out she is.*]

LULU: The revolution, you total idiot of poop smears, will be glorious. Hundreds of clowns, at the gates, their breasts bare, the colors of our oppressor ripped to shreds, the flags desecrated – we will unravel their emblem and smear our menstrual blood and shit on the very things they try to control. They try to control what is mine, my body, my words, my waste, it's not waste, it's how I work, that's how I work, why I am here – it's all rage!

KOKO: What then? What's the plan? You just build it back up to put you and your "sisters" back on top?

LULU: Oh what – and you'd just burn it all down? You'll get lost in the flames.

KOKO: I already am.

[*SOUND PERSON cues a harsh industrial sound mixed with the crash of a modern connection and the pounding of machines. Perhaps the sound emanates from the painting of the factory. LULU and KOKO cover their ears in pain until it passes, this time the length of a commercial, about 30 seconds.*]

TELEVISION PERSONALITY: And now after our commercial break we return to "Jailbreak!"*, Trademark!

LULU: Alright. [*Pause.*] Your story. Or whatever. Your turn. Doesn't have to be ... a narrative per se.

KOKO: I see it.

[*Agitation as LULU becomes alert.*]

LULU: What? A boat?!
KOKO: [*singing*] I see it in the distance.
LULU: A boat?
KOKO: [*finishing the hook from the Seashellz "I see it in the Distance."*] Woah oh oh.
LULU: [*completely deflated*] What?
KOKO: It's a song, you were talking about songs earlier. [*Pause.*] Ok. Fine. I see it in the distance, and it's a, uh, a story.
LULU: What's the story?
KOKO: Uhh ... there's two women. And they just broke out of jail.
LULU: That's really all you have right now?
KOKO: Ok uh – this mid-century modern table is inspired by elegant and glamorous designs of the Triassic period—
LULU: No SEO babble!
KOKO: [*Breath.*] I had the dream again last night.
LULU: Oh my word, this again? Koko, you repeat yourself – attempt invention!

KOKO: Shut up. I've prepared myself to repeat myself. [*Pause.*] It was a dream, a dream about my old house. See, my father and I visit... OK look, not all of this is going to be linear. So we park the car on the cul-de-sac. And by the time we are finished with the parking break and the car and everything, the sun is already setting. I rush into the backyard to catch the sunset and this – giant ball – hits the horizon. The sun is like fucking huge and the entire sky turns pink. And I am, like, in tears. This is one of the most overwhelming views in my life. And for no reason, my backyard, it comes up against the ocean, suddenly. And there's this new building behind my old house in the water. But, besides that, all I can see is the sky, like, baby blues, giant pink clouds like cotton candy, and the wavering, glowing sun. So I turn to the tour group that's, like, suddenly there for no reason, and I say to them, "I grew up with this," as I cry. They are all waving and clapping and smiling. And then the tour guide forces me and my daddy to get out of the way as darkness finally descends.

[*A moment passes.*]

LULU: Really? You are such a child. What do you want? Exactly? Today is the day we break free. Today is the day of our salvation.
KOKO: Salvation? And you accuse me of cursing Christ?
LULU: Is it just food you want in your belly?
KOKO: You know what I want? Let's go back. I want to go back to burn it down. Torch in hand. Giant burning trunk of tree.
LULU: You know why you want to go back? Because you want to be back in prison. Because you are a pussy. And prison is for pussies!

[*KOKO begins to cry.*]

55

LULU: Why you cry?

KOKO: Sandra. Did you see what they did to her?

LULU: [*Spits.*] Yeah. That was some gnarly shit.

KOKO: She wasn't even supposed to be in jail. Those motherfuckers – all they see is purple and green and a little clown smile, they don't see the person inside.

LULU: How long you even been a clown? Hmm? You aren't a real clown. You just wear that make up, smile real big, and do what the boss man tells you. You weren't born this way, you chose to be a clown.

KOKO: Oh you did not just say that.

[*KOKO strangles LULU.*]

KOKO: What's my name?

LULU: Koko!

KOKO: Yeah! Well uh – What's your name?

LULU: Lulu!

KOKO: Uhm – what's my name?

LULU: Koko!

KOKO: Are you sure?

LULU: Yes!

KOKO: You very sure?? Fine!

[*KOKO releases her stranglehold on LULU. KOKO smears her make-up off, but only about halfway.*]

KOKO: Yeah OK! We're not fucking clowns. No one's a fucking clown. Is that what you want to hear? No one's a fucking clown and no one's a fucking person. Until they, like, stamp it with that word, with that name that's floating over their head like a fucking identity card. So yeah, we ain't clowns anymore. No, we are just two losers caught here on the edge of the beach at the edge of the world so don't reproduce for me our fucked up society!!!

[*SOUND PERSON cues a harsh industrial sound mixed with the crash of a modem connection and the pounding of machines. Perhaps the sound emanates from the painting of the factory. LULU and KOKO cover their genitals in pain until it passes, this time about 20 seconds. SOUND PERSON increases the volume throughout until it is unbearable, forcing LULU and KOKO to quake uncontrollably. Finally they are released.*]

[*LULU and KOKO stand about. Their predicament remains unaltered.*]

LULU: Well perhaps we are going about it the wrong way, maybe there is an interior space, an auxiliary space.

KOKO: No, it's just the injuries that make it unbearable. Scar tissue.

LULU: That's what makes it possible! Scars drag you forward, actualities!

KOKO: It's all rhetoric with you!

LULU: Rhetoric is where real thought begins! Well, just beyond – beyond the shadow of that tree.

KOKO: Shut up! I can't stand your 2nd grade variety poetry!

LULU: No! It is how I will break free. Writing, not as a reflection of speaking, but as a process of fucking an erotic page with a wet pen, dripping ink down into her trimmed hairs.

KOKO: You aren't making any sense! You are just stringing words together, and it is pissing me off! Wasting your time with meters and line, [*realizing the trap*] GAH! It's like you're pissing in the wind!

LULU: That metaphor does not apply to REAL women! Piss all over yourself you fucked up hologram whore!

KOKO: You want liberty? Well then shut up and be free All-Read-E! Run! Drink rum! Finger bang your flappy cunt and cum! Lay under the sun! You don't need to talk about it to me.

LULU: No, that's what you want! I want liberty, you just want dick stroganoff – give or get a blow job, eat some fried scallops, blackened grouper, cream sauce on salmon – fuck job, cunt job, weekend warrior who needs a job—

KOKO: You know what the difference between you and me is?

LULU: Go ahead and enlighten me.

KOKO: I actually love my body.

LULU: Are you fucking kidding me? That, Koko, is a truly flabbergasting claim. Just look at what you've done to yourself.

KOKO: Yeah, take a good look. This is me. I know who am and I know what I like. Does that scare you?

LULU: What scares me is the power they wield, hidden everywhere, in words, in looks, in desire. If we can get to the Island of Mu and join my sisters...

KOKO: Then what? What's your plan? Fight for the rest of your life?

LULU: Yes! There's a struggle going on!

KOKO: I'm not gonna burn up my whole life in anger, not anymore.

LULU: Koko – listen to yourself. You are stuck in your thinking. Leave your past behind, stop recreating their fantasies!

KOKO: Fantasies? You are trying to escape to an island full of lesbians so you can write erotic political poetry – and you accuse me of living in a fantasy? You, Lulu the Lunatic, is telling moi, Koko Magnifique, all about living in a fantasy? [*Takes a breath*] Well right back at you sister.

LULU: I'm not your fucking sister!

KOKO: You know what? Fuck this. I don't believe you exist anymore. That's a fantasy I've had for a while I'm ready to make a reality.

[*KOKO takes off her boot while talking.*]

LULU: What the fuck do you mean?

KOKO: I don't believe you exist. I don't see why the fuck you are here! Always, always, always dragging me the other way.

LULU: What do you mean I don't exist, I'm right fucking here!

KOKO: It's like the torture never stops – I fucking jailbreak and you're still here!

[*KOKO brandishes her boot at LULU.*]

LULU: So what – you gonna kill me?

KOKO: And drag your ass around this beach handcuffed to my arm? No, I'm going to commit a different crime. Manifestation? I call it creation. I'm gonna make a new friend. If I wanna talk to somebody, I'm gonna talk to her.

[*KOKO takes off her ripped up sock that has a face on it. She creates a sock puppet, LALA – her new friend. She begins to talk to it.*]

LALA: Me OW!

KOKO: I'll never really burn up my past until I make believe up a future.

LALA: JEEESusssss Mother Fucking Christ and Mother Mary of God Mother Fucker!

[*KOKO gets on the ground with LALA and prepares to recreate her finest moment, her escape from prison.*]

KOKO: Keep Digging! Keep digging we're almost free!

LALA: Move your foot, you're stepping on my womb!

KOKO: Keep digging, keep pushing!

[*KOKO and LALA start digging a tunnel into the sand in the beach.*]

[*LULU stands, somehow alone yet still attached to the pair.*]

LULU: She's abandoned me.

[*KOKO and LALA fall into a rapid-fire rapport that is sometimes combative but more often supportive.*]

LALA: Mother Mary of Goddamit God Rape!
KOKO: Keep digging, sister!
LALA: Mother Jesus Creep!

LULU: I'm all alone. Ha! And why not? Why do I, Lulu, need someone to talk to after all? Talking is for pussies!

LALA: Hell! Hell hell hell!
KOKO: Keep digging, keep pushing, we are about to break free!
This is a Jailbreak, Trademark!

LULU: It's up to me to discover the plan, the plan to absolute liberty. And there's only one way.
It's not talking...
I've got to start writing

[*LULU hunkers down with her pen and the Chinese take-out menu/map. She begins scrawling.*]

KOKO: Keep digging, little puppet person!
LALA: Shut up and hand me that used diaper and that pair of crocodile teeth! Iz gotz a plan!
KOKO: Thank God! No more running through the tunnels like a plague rat.
LALA: Or worse the fleas on a plague rat.
KOKO: And no more burrowing looking for a peek of light.
LALA: One sniff of something other than the stench of urine, bile, vomit, and decay.

LULU: I will write the words that will live free of their
       envelopes, causation and time! I follow the trail of
       the hand leaving its trace. No head, not even a
       bladder and intestines – only hands! Leaving an ink
       trace like a trail of bullets, an arc aimed like a
       rocket!

KOKO: Gonna burn that memory, my life in the stupid city.
LALA: Never gonna go back to your little bitty witty box.
KOKO: All that chitter chatter and the pumpity dump.
LALA: Fuck that chat chat chattering in the dark and let us
       dig a hole!

LULU: For we now the hand for to the crime! Endless
       crime, crime out, snapping lungs not snorting I
       reverse choke out predicate parts, assault and revolt
       on grammar.

KOKO: No more television characters, shuffling up and
       down the stairs trying to catch a subway train.
LALA: Domiciles like prison cells, Internet streaming
       security camera in your work machine.
KOKO: Watching me shit, shower, and shave my goddamn
       little pube-ees.

LULU: Undigested apex of undwindled thought balloons
       fucking softly belly flesh – Pedo-rape-itron! I crime
       it out! Crime and crime again to subsist and live on
       rhyme!

[*SOUND PERSON cues gunfire. Gunshots start slowly from far off,
increasing until the sound of machine guns are near. LULU begins
choking and gagging, grabbing her belly and neck in a mixture of pain
and hunger. She slows down, gasping out her words as she moves toward
death.*]

LULU: A crime of the mind that eclipses all signs,
collapsing all borders into a liquid storm, a
dangerous weather system and I will strike the page
– like lightning!

LALA: I see the glassy surface of the prison walls – all thick
with mirror tongues flapping out the jailers' calls.

KOKO: Little happy emoticons, sun and moon with
dull pixel eyes. Burn it with a burning tree, a
tree that I bite just to hear it bleed.

LALA: In the shadow of the past is the path straight back
to jail, fall into the shadow of a burning tree instead.

KOKO: Yeah, because a tree is a monster organism, a
monster just like us, with no fucking hands.

LULU: I storm (hack hack) and (hack cough hack) rage
(hack hack hack).

LALA: We burn ye and you won't steal our voice, we won't
make a lost call into the night!

KOKO: Instead I make contact, invention straight from the
womb, gonna burn bright!

[*LULU dies in absolute agony with a horrible sound as gunfire
increases to a manic rate.*]

LALA: It's just you and me and a little bitty play with a
firecracker ending, I dream the images and you
bring them into being.

KOKO: Yeah, and we will get a hundred clowns together
and they'll read off your writing!

LALA: No, not a hundred. 117 precisely, and they'll have to
count them!

KOKO: And also a dog with a tuxedo on a tricycle barking
and eating shit at the same time.

LALA: While countless dicks get fucked into one giant
        pussy that's gobbling up the moon.
KOKO: And all the trees sway and are blind and can see at
        the same time.
LALA: And food, Koko! A giant mountain of food that no
        one eats because it's just coins and the coins all start
        spinning.
KOKO: And the curtain opens and closes and opens and
        closes, making all the audience dizzy.
LALA: Except the audience is all putting on their own
        plays and they all have to make their own puppets –
KOKO: Fuck it! I know all about liberty! I'm gonna dig us
        free! Burn in hell!

[*KOKO stands triumphant. Suddenly, industrial sounds mixed with
modem crash come in. KOKO freezes, confused. Time rewinds,
restarting at the moment LULU begins writing about envelopes.*]

LULU: I will write the words that will live free of their
        envelopes, causation and time! I follow the trail of
        the hand leaving its trace. No head, not even a
        bladder and intestines – only hands! Leaving an ink
        trace like a trail of bullets, an arc aimed like a
        rocket!

KOKO: Gonna burn that memory, my life in the stupid city.
LALA: Never gonna go back to your little bitty witty box.
KOKO: All that chitter chatter and the pumpity dump.
LALA: Fuck that chat chat chattering in the dark and dig a
        hole!

LULU: For we now the hand for to the crime! Endless
        crime, crime out, snapping lungs not snorting I
        reverse choke out predicate parts, assault and revolt
        on grammar.

KOKO: No more television characters, shuffling up and
down the stairs trying to catch a subway train.

LALA: Domiciles like prison cells, Internet streaming
security camera in your work machine.

KOKO: Watching me shit, shower, and shave my goddamn
little pube-ees.

LULU: Undigested apex of undwindled thought balloons
fucking softly belly flesh – Pedo-rape-itron! I crime
it out! Crime and crime again to subsist and live on
rhyme. A crime of the mind that eclipses all signs,
collapsing all borders into a liquid storm, a
dangerous weather system and I will strike the page
like lightning!

LALA: I see the glassy surface of the prison walls – all thick
with mirror tongues flapping out the (cough
cough) jailers' (hack hack) calls!

[SOUND PERSON cues gunfire. Gunshots start slowly from far off,
increasing until the sound of machine guns are near. KOKO and LALA
start to cough and hack as they speak while gunshots start to ring out.
KOKO grabs her stomach in pain – gunshot or hungry, we cannot tell.]

KOKO: Little happy emoticons, sun and moon with
dull pixel eyes. Burn it with a burning tree, a
tree that I bite just to hear it bleed.

LALA: In the shadow of the past is the path straight back
to [vomits loudly] jail, fall into the shadow of a
burning tree instead.

[KOKO falls to the ground.]

KOKO: Yeah because a tree is a monster organism, a monster just like us.

LULU: I storm and rage, not like a single silver lined cloud, not like all the weather ever, but as the weather, as and is, forever! I am the weather? No, I have no I, no eye nor eyes, weather mates divine – and crime!!

KOKO: With no (hack hack hack) fucking (hack cough hack) hands (hack hack hack).

LULU: I will commit the perfect crime, against all jailers, against the giant penis of my sovereign, the Father Mask, and against all the women that would be cuckolded by the words they martyr us to like crucifixes fashioned from road signs.

[*KOKO dies horribly, with a loud sound of wretching.*]

LALA: Hands! Only hands!

[*LALA THE PUPPET dies with a horrible sound as gunfire increases.*]

LULU: The hand strikes! Sight of divine rhyme when discovering the currents that tie and then strikes – goodbye! We will break free with our tools, the tools left over from our torture! The rotten smell of vowels and nonsense streaming out of my orifices, undigested excrement from my little eyelets that open to reveal boats full of naked refugee miscreants covered in profanity laced to their blood and bone, all on that razor thin page – but by Satan only when you write. Don't write the write you think you write, just write and it will be all right. Raising the chisel high, I see the silhouette on the wall – it is the dream ones, my father's vapor – fuck that pig! No more grammar, no more sound, no more speaking, no more songs or rhymes, only writing trace of traces of translation into and out of these patriarchal controlling word balloons! Bastards! There must be some way out! Keep digging sister!

[*LULU turns to the corpse of KOKO to offer encouragement. Gunshots increase to a frenzy. Now neither LULU nor KOKO is alive or dead. When either LULU or KOKO speaks, standing, triumphant, the other is dead on the ground. They continue to alternate, jumping up and down, both alive and dead, but never at the same time. KOKO continues to speak with her puppet but only loosely. Over the gunfire, SOUND PERSON cues a canned recording of "Taps" played by a military bugle.*]

KOKO: I'm free I'm free I'm free!
LULU: Liberty! Lib Er Tee!
KOKO: I see a tree that bleeds!
LULU: It's only ever me!
KOKO: We made it to the sea!
LULU: I have no eyes to see!
KOKO: Oh boy oh joy oh wee!
LULU: I wrote an immortal creed!
KOKO: I'm free I'm blee I'm klee!
LULU: Bye Hi Rye We Ray Mi!
KOKO: I've achieved final ecstasy!
LULU: I collapse into infinity!

[*Finally both LULU and KOKO die. They drop down dead next to each other, still handcuffed. "Taps" plays out, followed by the whistling of a bomb falling. The whistling becomes deafening, and then suddenly stops. No explosion. All sound stops except the sound of the beach.*]

[*SOUND PERSON comes out from his/her station with watering can and flowers (large daisies or sunflowers). The flowers are thrown carelessly on the corpses of LULU and KOKO. SOUND PERSON tips the watering can and waters the flowers on the corpses.*]

SOUND PERSON: There's your goddamn plurality. "The End!"

[*LULU and KOKO sit up holding the flowers, both humans and plants revived by the water.*]

LULU AND KOKO: Ta-da!

CURTAIN

BONUS

LEVEL

The Creation of the Clowniverse
For Pochinko

Below
Tallahassee, FL
Tuesday, November 3rd, 2020

Clowns in our government and clowns in the pulpit. Clowns in parades and clowns in exposes. Clowns on T.V. and clowns in the streets. Clowns in adverts and clowns in campaigns. Historical clowns, performing clowns, acrobatic clowns, stupid clowns, DMT clowns, murder clowns, clowns rapping or raping, happy clowns, sad clowns, clowns in the cinema, and clowns in books.

What *is* it about clowns?

It is late Tuesday evening in the capital of Florida. They are counting the votes district by district, county by county, to discover: Who will be the winner? All the votes must be counted first, hanging chads or not, put in machines, collated, collected, and finally graphed and compared to the predictions of statisticians. The denizens of this strange peninsula, long tongue of limestone submerging itself in the rising ocean like some cranky alligator, await the verdict.

Yet something unexpected starts to happen. The data for Sarasota county is next in line for the counting. Here is the home of the great clown schools, the great clown graveyards, the great clown museums. Statues of clowns adorn the streets of downtown. John Ringling's estate hosts tours with expert guides explaining the many clowns of Sarasota history. And on this late Tuesday, the clowns begin to murmur. The clowns deep in the dirt, beneath the ground. The clowns in the paintings, in the long halls of the Cà d'Zan. The clowns in the circus, the clowns in the toy shops, the clowns on display down Pineapple street.

The votes are prepared for counting. The clowns begin murmuring, now whispering, now speaking. What do they want? To be counted? No, what they want is to speak; they want to be heard. And what will they say over the din of information? The graphs of all the ballots? The blaring noise of the historical record? The crushing weight of all the books in the Selby library? What can they possibly say to be heard over the pummeling stream of the Internet?

What will they say to make you laugh? To make you think?

For a moment the ballots are put aside. Everyone turns to the clowns and wait. The clowns open their mouths. It is the Creation of the Clowniverse.

East
New York, NY
Friday, October 30th, 2015

Socrates walks into a bar in the basement of the Bohemian Grove. Behind the bar, Lily and I are dressed up like presents, all bows, bells, and garish patterns. I am wearing a tight-fitting knit cotton dress with red and black stripes. The dress follows the contours of my hips and my black bra is overstuffed with socks full of rice. I have liberally applied foundation, obscuring my five o'clock shadow. Lily and I are wearing her expensive lipsticks with names like crimson pink and moth blue.

Socrates has come to this party, the late night Glitter Factory, searching for truth. He has questions that must be answered. Where was God when De Soto hacked his way through the Florida underbrush? Is consciousness an energy field that extends beyond the limits of the material body? What would grammar say if it could stand up and speak or is predicate logic a parasite? Why did that play he just saw quote liberally from the ancient Chinese classic the Book of Songs?

But first Socrates orders a drink. Lily and I fix him a cocktail in a red Solo cup. "Try this," we say, offering him the cup. "What's it called?" he asks. "Creation of the Clowniverse," we answer. He drinks the hemlock and becomes myth.

West
Los Angeles, CA
Friday, October 31st, 2014

I am writing a book while living in a closet in a small, dimly lit apartment off Firmin Street in Echo Park. The book is about an American politician and double mastectomy survivor named the Statesman. She is conspiring with the Russian government to create a hoax, to dupe the world into thinking there is a second Cold War through a series of dummy Internet start-ups in Eastern Europe. The story is also about an art thief (known as "the Thief") banished from America for pedophilia and sodomy. In one scene, the Statesman and the Thief consume a plant extract given to them by the Statesman's daughter, a performance art MFA candidate at your local college. Once consumed, all three of them are sucked into the Clowniverse. The following scene then takes place:

Error and Mayhem are two LSD clowns wandering a place called Trash City. They are aimlessly drifting on the hazy exhaust trails of some burnt-out party favors in a cascading regress one long Halloween night. Error is dressed as a third-eye pirate, Mayhem is dressed as a jungle freak. Their clothes are cheap, their makeup smears in the rain, and they cannot stop laughing. They find themselves in a pink psychedelic dungeon that oscillates and pulsates with the smell of sweat and cheap beer. Lace and silk adorn a constant flow of bodies, the material cut to reveal shaved skin: a nipple here, a bellybutton there, the flowering crack of an ass or the mushroom tip of a penis. Hues of pigment more varied than the colors of the desert. Bare earlobes listening to the paintings vibrate. A naked woman writhes on the ground in careful choreography to the sound of feedback, performed by a cadre of denim-clad teenagers.

Outside, Error and Mayhem giggle uncontrollably as their tobacco becomes moist and clumpy in the rain, their rolling papers splitting apart. A hooligan with a nose full of Adderall dust and a beret cocked on his head accosts the two clowns. He pulls out a digital device, shows them Instagram photos of still existing graffiti conquests. This speed-talking madman draws closer to Error, babbling of assassination plots, of secret revolutionary symbols originating from the Tompkins Square riots. He draws pictures of these glyphs and writes the name of hooligan crews, boy-gangs named after orifices, committed vandals. "I have learned the first language." He draws a letter, an ancient rune you might have seen on a stone adorning an old road. "And I've drawn it everywhere. I've even written it on the walls of Sarasota, Florida, inside the abandoned Ringling towers – yes, I was there, trespassing before they were demolished." He leans in close and whispers, "I am a poet and I've read Harry Crews."

With that, he quickly pats Error's penis through his jeans and disappears into the party through a door glowing pink with artificial light. Cops suddenly arrive to break up the evening, pushing through the door in pairs. Error and Mayhem look sideways, turn, and wander away from the party while whistling nondescriptly. They turn the wrong way in the rain and wander deep into Chinatown. Error keeps imagining the pink door, wondering what would have followed if he had stepped through. What, eggzactly, would be the next turn in the story? Then – an epiphany. Door or no door, *this* is the Creation of the Clowniverse.

South
The Sacred Territories, GA
Saturday, June 21st, 2014

I take the dose of the sacred medicine on the summer solstice. A clown named Chicken, a beautiful woman from Tybee Island and a close friend, takes the dose with me. We wander into the Georgia wilderness where the clay is as orange as the smile of a clown. We are led by Gunter, who guides a whole troop of us pilgrims deep into the woods. We are headed to the Goddess Garden where our departed friend Cornbread once worshipped while he still lived in Palookaville. This trip will take an entire afternoon. I leave the procession for a moment and sit on the top of a ridge, squatting among the chiggers, watching the line of my friends snake through the woods on the skinny trail. Suddenly, I am beside them, standing on one leg on top of a log. "Oh!" Chicken exclaims. "I thought you had disappeared. How did you get there?"

As we burrow deeper into the woods, I imagine myself bringing my clown theater troop out here. I imagine the Saints of an Unnamed Country performing our plays deep in the Sacred Territories, presenting our works to the trees. We would unveil our fabled Kabbalist classic, The Colossus. In this theatrical endeavor, Pantalone and il Dottore construct a golem from the wedding vows of their respective children. The golem is built to beat a hole in the ground. The hole is made to divert a river, the run-off from a Glacier, and keep it from flooding their little town of Colossae. By doing so, Pantalone and il Dottore accidentally recreate the quantity zero, the empty space.

As I contemplate this, we weave through the woods, past Stumblebum creek, past the distillery. Now I am imagining Cornbread at the end of his life, spending his time reading and writing poetry. I imagine sitting in his slender apartment, the smell of whiskey and cigarettes long gone – his deteriorating health necessitates abstaining from such vices. I imagine us discussing our shared love of Shakespeare and comparing stories of our families and our fathers, the source of all drama. We would discuss Shakespeare's family, how his drama changed as he aged deeper into family life. I imagine Cornbread in his glasses and beret, his dour face, his world-weary demeanor, his devotion to poetry.

We arrive at the Goddess Garden. We stand in a circle among the idols. Gunter presents a clear plastic bag full of Cornbread's ashes. The bag is passed around the circle and each person sprinkles his ashes onto the dirt of the garden. I abstain. As the bag passes me by in its journey around the circle, a shaft of light breaks through the overcast sky. Next, a glass decanter of tequila with a long, narrow spout is passed around the circle of friends. To drink, each of us must kneel while the person next in line pours the tequila from the decanter into our mouth. In time, we are all thoroughly intoxicated, choking on the tequila as our partners forget to stop pouring.

The woods darken in the span of a moment. The wind gathers and a storm rolls in. I am reminded of my childhood in Florida, the heavy rains suddenly appearing each afternoon. And I am reminded of Cornbread repeating his brother's warning: "Don't die. I can't afford to bury you." I opened my play "The Storm" with those words. As the woods darken, I feel Cornbread with us, not as a ghost, but as a memory, a myth. Just like the memory of weather from my youth.

Gunter chases into the storm with Lucifer, his dog. Megawatt, another denizen of the Sacred Territories, chases after him and I follow close behind. Chicken and the others turn back. Megawatt and I wind down the ridge, the rain heavy now. We crawl through blackberry bushes. At the bottom of the ridge, and onto a branching trail, we find Gunter down in the swamp, sitting alone, quiet, on the wooden bridge. We all sit together for a moment, staring in the crick. I reach into my pocket, take out my cigarettes, and throw them away. We all do. But it is an empty gesture. We do not quit that day.

No, we sit up all night back at the W.G., hanging out by the stove, drinking beers and smoking, laughing our heads off. Gunter, Megawatt, Chicken, and I are planning to perform a play.

The play will take place at an old haunted house in Atlanta, the last place Cornbread was living. In the play, an old man is slowly dying, obsessed with dreams of his youth, obsessed with a memory of the moon as a raven. A drunk clown transcribes everything said by this man, this would be Emperor. We laugh as we plan this play. It was called "The Emperor & the Moon." It might as well have been called "The Creation of the Clowniverse."

North
East Glacier, MT
10,000 B.C.

Three clowns are stuffed like rubber chickens into a red clown car with a stick shift and a hatchback. Primary colors like Blue, Taupe, and Syblam adorn their garments as a signal of gaiety and cultivated madness. They are scooting their vehicle across the Continental Divide, northward toward the Canadian border. They are starving for want of food, gasoline, and fresh underwear. They left long behind the cinema eye, blinking this and that way, cutting off limbs. All they retain is their songs and stories of songs they might write together.

They are scooting down the highway in their little car, traveling from one melting glacier in the Tetons to another melting glacier in the Crown of the Continent. On their way, on a particularly long road out of Missoula headed in the wrong direction, they discuss the origin and meaning of the Clowniverse.

"It began sometime in early 2014, during that week in New Orleans leading up to Mardi Gras—"

"No, a little before that, when methane began escaping in the Arctic Circle at an ever more alarming rate—"

"No, a bit before, in 2012, on the streets of Baltimore, that clown holding the window, a sombrero on his head—"

"No, it was in the early 19ᵗʰ century when Grimaldi made his name in the Harlequinade—"

...and so on and so forth...

"There are real, historical, Egyptian clowns!"

"Birds masquerading as clowns came to Elijah!"

"The first one to speak in history was immediately followed by the laughter of a clown!"

...all the way back through history, to the empty space that precedes the beginning.

One thing they all agree on is the number. There is a consensus on the number three, just as there are three clowns in the car. It may begin with two (which two we could not say), but it never ends there. At the very least, one more clown is bound to show up. A good clown story cannot end until there are at least three clowns. On this one facet of the Clowniverse they can all agree.

Later, they sit around a campfire in East Glacier. They hold sticks and roast pork weenies over the flames. They look up to the mountains and they see one patch of ice broken apart like an egg over a frying pan, water running down from the edges, cutting long rivulets in the steps of the mountain wall. They stare in awful/awesome awe through the smoke of their campfire as they discern a figure trotting out from this melting field of ice. It is the glacier itself. It walks down the mountain, neither quick nor slow. Soon, it stands in front of their campsite, about seven feet tall, very erect, and made entirely of ice. Bipedal but inhuman.

It speaks with a voice that booms over the hills, "You people! You demons of fire, of energy escaping! Your waste has loosened me like a cup of coffee on the bowels, and I will run down the mountains and drown your future in lakes and oceans! In rivers of rising water! I will sink and drown your Florida and steal from you all that belongs to you including your birthright. Coral Gables and the alligators of the Everglades. Siesta Key and Turtle Beach. All this I claim as my own."

The clowns huddle closer together on one side of the orange

fire as the walking glacier melts before them, escaping into the air and into the soil in equal measure. They turn to each other, looking for some response, some answer. Something to say in the silence. Simultaneously, they all open their mouths and laugh. In that moment, they do it again. They recreate the empty space, redraw the sign for the quantity zero. They name it the Creation of the Clowniverse.

Above
Highway 1, CA
Sunday, December 25th, 2016

Richard Brautigan and Jack Spicer walk into a clown bar. They are both asshole alcoholics. They both order whiskey cocktails. The name of the cocktail is the F.G. Lorca. They smell horrible as they lean against the bar, smell like burnt toast jumping out of an appliance and into the San Francisco bay. As they talk and drink, they share poems, stories.

In one story they never bothered to write down, a canyon opens up in New Mexico and swallows a bird, burps a few ghosts out. Clowns cross over the canyon on tightropes, carefully taking notes. Silent thieving losers, perpetually broke, drained of everything but a single color that slashes across bone white complexions. They are adorned with painted diamonds like the markings of demons. None of their clothes fit.

The clowns return to the beginning of the trail. Morphemes dangle and drip from the corners of their mouths, phonemes stain the seats of their pants. Ghost trees stand silently on the rim of the canyon, their voices robbed by drought and infestation. The clowns climb back into their clown car. The air crackles with carbon. Windshield wipers flick against the glass, pushing the soot and ash aside. The clowns hydrate from a plastic bottle, the final ration in their water supply.

I sit in a house off Highway 1 and stare at the Pacific Ocean from a window. I read the books of long dead San Franciscans. They are monks of serial thinking in writing. Maybe not monks. Certainly not chaste. Wet with desire. For love, for drink, for trout. All their books are letters written back and forth.

I am writing an introduction to a book of plays. I leave my phone in the house and take a walk on the bluffs of Gualala. I stop on a craggy outcropping to watch the sun sink into the ocean. Down the bluffs, I see a seagull watching as well. When the orange orb disappears, the bird flies away.

Back at the house, a vaporizer and a bottle of scotch make the rounds. I abstain. Well, not from the scotch. I am trying to stay focused despite my phone lying near. I open a black composition book and try to write. Perhaps I will write a poem for the autumnal holidays. But the fall is over. Autumn ends and winter, the savior, begins. It is Christmas today and we are celebrating the birth of the King. Who will be king next year? I wonder. The elected leaders of the world laugh at me from televisions, magazines, and phone applications. And who will speak to the king of his failings? Who will speak with immunity? Only the fool can speak such things.

I think of my nephew and niece in Florida. They are celebrating with my family: my brother and his wife, my father and my mother. I think of the two little children. How will they speak when the time comes? How will they be heard over the din of collapsing systems everywhere? Over the sound of waves crashing higher and higher on the shore? How will they speak with salt water in their lungs and nothing to drink?

I want to give them the speaking. Instead, I write them a letter. This is the letter. I put it inside an envelope. Alongside the letter, inside the envelope, is the Creation of the Clowniverse.

My Clown Mask
Sarasota, FL
Sunday, December 22nd, 1985

The first time I was ever on stage I played Santa Claus. I was two-years old and I talked my way into a production of the Night Before Christmas that was being staged at a department store. "We need a volunteer!" I raised my hand. They called me onto the stage. "He's too small." I smiled. I grinned. They gave me the red suit. I walked on stage and got in place. I watched the man in his kerchief sleeping. I watched him through the window of the set. And when I laughed as he dozed, my belly shook like a bowl full of jelly. I know because they gave me plastic fruit to stuff the middle of my suit, and I would grab and shake my paunch as I laughed.

The first memory in my brain is my little blue room. It is the room I was born into in Sarasota, Florida. The room was filled with little clown dolls. They wore silver and gold garments, little pointy hats, with big smiles and curly hair. They hung from lamps, from the curtains, from the corners of things, looking at me and grinning. A stuffed unicorn sat in the corner. On the wall hung a cowboy depicted in yarn instead of paint, with a brown hat and a red bandana. These were my friends.

I remember the frame of my bed. I remember the shape of my dresser. I remember the window and I remember the view. I remember the plastic shade and the light peeking through, light from the yard, full of big trees with red berries. Trees perfect for climbing. I couldn't sleep through that peeking light so we eventually taped the shade to the frame of the window.

I loved my room, loved that house, loved being inside of it, loved the color of the blue walls. Still, I dream of that room, I dream I return to it. Once I dreamed I came back with my father, and we saw the sun set in the backyard, no longer a pasture beyond the fence, but somehow, magically, the Gulf of Mexico. In my dreams, I return to my origin, to the beginning of my story, a little blue room full of toys and smiling clowns. It is the Creation of the Clowniverse.

END

THE

About The Author

Cameron Christopher Stuart and Seraphic Romance Rots Truth is a playwright, poet, and storyteller. He is the founder of the theater company Saints of an Unnamed Country. Born in Sarasota, Florida, he now lives in Brooklyn, New York.

Other Titles Available from

A Freedom Books:

Stephanie B., *Letters To Aunt Lucy, Chapter 1*. AFB010.

Marshall Deerfield, *Travel By Haiku, Volumes 1-5: Still Trippin' Across The States*. AFB011.

Marshall James Kavanaugh, *Fire. Sun. Salutation.* AFB007

Sage Kohen, *Seeds of Illumination*, AFB012

Morrison Willow, *Borderline Fictions*. AFB006.

Willow Zef, *Birds & Commas*. AFB008.

spread it

afreedombooks.com

End Credits

Cover and Book Design by Cameron Christopher Stuart with Marshall James Kavanaugh.

"THE END" photos by Stephanie Beattie (*City of Songs*) and Mallie Sanford ("*Jailbreak*!"*tm).

Author photo by Mallie Sanford.

92840256R00062

Made in the USA
Columbia, SC
05 April 2018